REAL WORLD DATA

GRAPHING HEALTH AND DISEASE

Barbara A. Somervill

Chicago, Illinois

www.heinemannraintree.com
Visit our website to find out
more information about
Heinemann-Raintree books.

To order:
☎ Phone 888-454-2279
▣ Visit www.heinemannraintree.com
to browse our catalog and order online.

Edited by Megan Cotugno and Diyan Leake
Designed by Victoria Bevan and Geoff Ward
Original illustrations © Capstone Global Library, LLC 2010
Illustrated by Geoff Ward
Picture research by Mica Brancic, Q2AMedia
Originated by Chroma Graphics (Overseas) Pte L:td
Printed in China by Leo Paper Products Ltd

14 13 12 11 10
10 9 8 7 6 5 4 3 2 1

Library of Congress Cataloging-in-Publication Data
Somervill, Barbara A.
 Graphing health and disease / Barbara A. Somervill.
    p. cm. -- (Real world data)
 Includes bibliographical references and index.
  ISBN 978-1-4329-2619-9 (hc) -- ISBN 978-1-4329-2628-1
(pb) 1. Health--Charts, diagrams, etc. 2. Diseases--Charts,
diagrams, etc. I. Title.
  RA776.5.S66 2008
  616.0022'2--dc22
                          2009001187

Acknowledgments
The author and publishers are grateful to the following for
permission to reproduce copyright material:
Alamy p. **9** (BennettPhoto); Corbis p. **27** (Inden/zefa);
Dreamstime p. **10** (Photoeuphoria); Fotolia p. **6** (AVAVA);
iStockphoto pp. **16** (Mark Hatfield), **21** (© Marcelo Wain);
Public Health Image Library p. **8**; Science Photo Library
p. **14** (Sam Ogden); Shutterstock pp. **4** (Julián Rovagnati),
15 (Sebastian Kaulitzki), **19** (Shipov Oleg), **22** (Jakub Cejpek),
24 (Andresr); © USDA Center for Nutrition Policy and
Promotion p. **25**.

Cover photograph of children receiving polio vaccination
in Kabul, Afghanistan reproduced with permission of AP
(Empics/Tomas Munita).

We would like to thank Dr. Michelle Raabe for her invaluable
help in the preparation of this book.

Every effort has been made to contact copyright holders
of any material reproduced in this book. Any omissions
will be rectified in subsequent printings if notice is given
to the publisher.

All the Internet addresses (URLs) given in this book were
valid at the time of going to press. However, due to the
dynamic nature of the Internet, some addresses may have
changed, or sites may have changed or ceased to exist since
publication. While the author and Publishers regret any
inconvenience this may cause readers, no responsibility
for any such changes can be accepted by either the author
or the Publishers.

CONTENTS

Some words are printed in bold, **like this**. You can find out what they mean by looking in the glossary, on page 30.

WHAT IS GOOD HEALTH?

The way to keep a body healthy is to develop good health habits. Think of the body as a machine. It needs fuel and care to keep it working smoothly. The fuels a body needs are food and water. The care it needs is plenty of sleep or rest and exercise.

Eating well is an important step in having good health. This means eating a mixed diet of vegetables and fruits, grains, and **proteins**. Not eating enough of these or eating too much sugar or fat is not good for the body. The human body also needs plenty of water. Many people do not drink enough water. A lack of water is called **dehydration**. It makes the body feel tired. Dehydration can cause headaches and, when severe, damage **organs**.

What are graphs?
This book uses graphs to show information about health and disease. Graphs show information or data visually. There are many different types of graphs, but all graphs make it easier to quickly see patterns.

 The human body needs a variety of nutritious foods to keep it healthy.

Bar graphs

The table below lists the **life expectancy** from birth in 12 nations. The bar graph below shows the same information in visual form. You can see that Japan has the highest life expectancy rate. Zimbabwe and Nigeria have the lowest on this list.

Country	Life Expectancy (in years from birth)	Country	Life Expectancy (in years from birth)
Australia	80.6	Japan	81.4
Brazil	72.2	Nigeria	47.4
China	72.9	Russia	65.9
Denmark	78.0	UK	78.7
India	68.6	U.S.	78.0
Iran	70.6	Zimbabwe	39.5

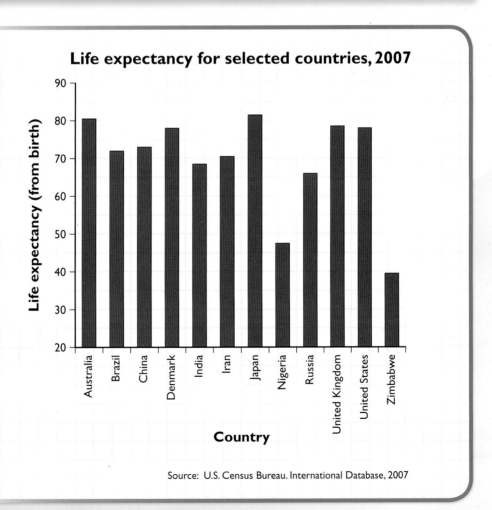

Life expectancy for selected countries, 2007

Source: U.S. Census Bureau. International Database, 2007

Disease or illness is the opposite of good health. Disease can come from many sources. Some diseases are caused by **microbes**, such as **bacteria** or **viruses**. Microbes or germs are in the air, food, and water. Germs enter the body when we breathe them in, eat or drink them, or when they enter through cuts on the body.

Types of disease

A disease that spreads from one person to another is called a **communicable** or **contagious** disease. These are diseases people can "catch," such as colds, measles, or HIV/AIDS. A doctor may test a sample of a patient's blood or **urine** to find out what causes a person's illness.

 Looking at blood or urine through a microscope can help doctors determine what is making a person sick.

Diseases that do not spread from one person to another are called **non-communicable**. Heart disease and cancer are non-communicable diseases. People do not "catch" heart disease from other people who have heart disease.

Sometimes people are born with a disease or the likelihood of developing disease. An example of a disease someone is born with is called a **congenital** disease. PKU (phenylketonuria) is a congenital disease that prevents a person's body from completely breaking down the protein

he or she eats. Children can also **inherit** disease in their **genes**. PKU is an inherited disease as well as a congenital disease. Sickle cell anemia and cystic fibrosis are other inherited diseases.

People who live in **developed countries** are far more likely to get heart disease or cancer than people in **developing countries**. People in developing countries are more likely to get HIV/AIDS, cholera, or measles. Where and how people live influences the diseases they might suffer during their lives.

Pie charts

Pie charts can be useful in comparing parts of a whole. An item that makes up a larger slice of the "pie" is a larger part of the whole. The pie charts below compare the main causes of death in developed and developing regions. In developed areas such as the U.S., more people die of non-communicable conditions, whereas communicable diseases are more significant in developing regions.

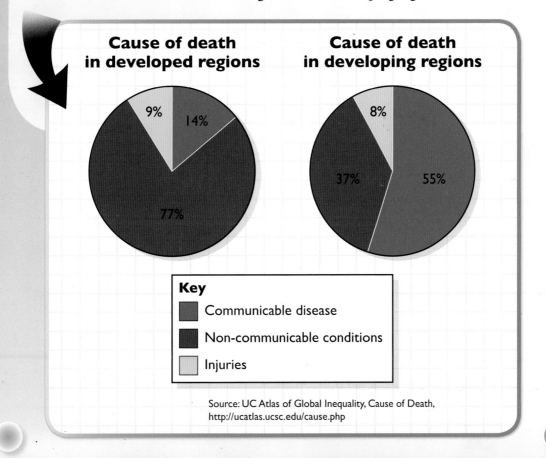

Cause of death in developed regions

9% 14% 77%

Cause of death in developing regions

8% 37% 55%

Key
- Communicable disease
- Non-communicable conditions
- Injuries

Source: UC Atlas of Global Inequality, Cause of Death, http://ucatlas.ucsc.edu/cause.php

COMMUNICABLE DISEASES

Throughout history, contagious diseases have been responsible for killing many millions of people. **Black Death** swept around the globe starting in the 1300s, killing more than 100 million people in 200 years. In 1918–1919, Spanish flu killed 50–100 million people in just two years. Today, HIV/AIDS is a contagious disease with a very high death rate. Since 1985, more than 25 million people have died of AIDS or AIDS-related diseases. Three million people die from AIDS-related illnesses each year.

Not all communicable diseases are deadly. Viruses cause colds, chicken pox, and measles. For most people, these illnesses cause fever and aches, but not death.

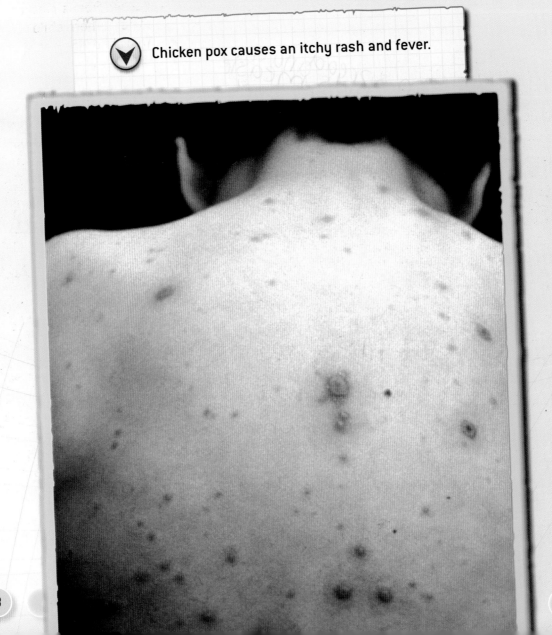

Chicken pox causes an itchy rash and fever.

Catching diseases

Communicable diseases are passed by being in contact with an **infected** person. The viruses that cause colds, flu, and chicken pox are passed by close contact with an infected person. This could include breathing in a cough or sneeze, or touching an object that has been contaminated with these viruses, such as a doorknob. HIV/AIDS is spread in body fluids, such as blood or **semen**. People do not catch HIV/AIDS from handshakes or coughing.

Some diseases can be carried in food or water. What most people call food poisoning is usually illness from bacteria. Eating infected food may cause vomiting, pain, or fever. Salmonellosis and *Escherichia coli* (*E. coli*) are two infections people get from eating infected food. Dirty drinking water may also be infected with diseases, such as cholera.

 The HIV virus can be passed from a mother to her unborn child. This child was born HIV-positive.

HIV and AIDS

HIV stands for "human immunodeficiency virus." AIDS stands for "acquired immunodeficiency syndrome." These are big words that represent a major worldwide **epidemic**

People infected with HIV are called HIV positive. HIV damages the immune system, the part of the body that prevents sickness. More than 42 million people live with HIV. If their disease becomes severe they are said to have AIDS. Their bodies cannot fight disease. HIV-positive people do not die from the virus but from other diseases they get because their immune system has been destroyed. **Tuberculosis** is a common cause of death in HIV-positive people.

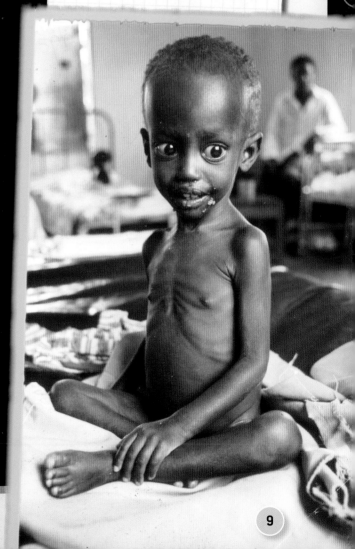

Immune system

The human body has its own immune system. It has special **cells**, body tissues, proteins, and organs to fight off disease. When people get sick, their bodies send white blood cells, called leukocytes, to fight the **infection**.

Some diseases, such as measles, can infect each human body only once. After a person has had measles, that person's blood makes special proteins, called **antibodies**. Antibodies stop the body from getting measles again.

 Flu shots help ward off the flu. For people who still get the flu, the shot makes it less serious.

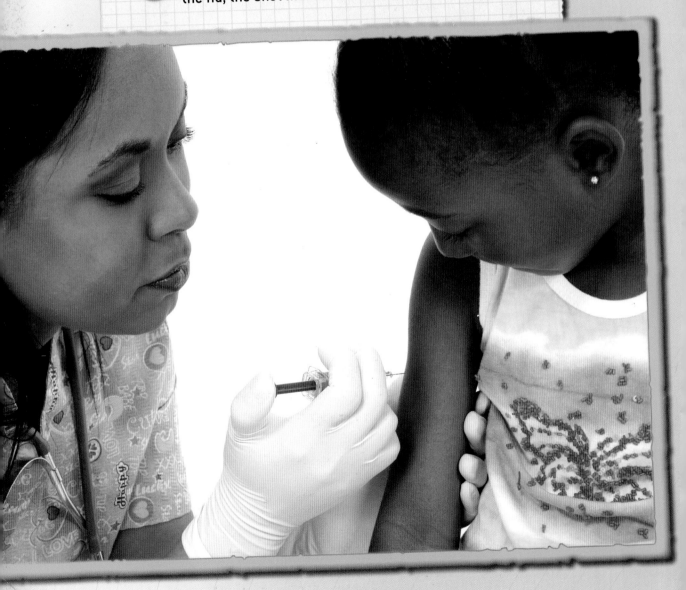

Vaccinations

More than 200 years ago, scientists noticed that if people survived some diseases, they never got those diseases again. Scientists wanted to find a way to prevent people from getting certain diseases to begin with. They developed **vaccines** that work much like a disease. For example, children get shots for MMR, which stands for measles, mumps, and rubella (German measles). The MMR vaccine encourages the body to make antibodies against measles, mumps, and rubella. The antibodies prevent the body from getting those diseases.

Scientists continue to work on developing new vaccines. Because of **immunizations**, most developed countries have few, if any, cases of what used to be common communicable diseases. Developing countries, where medical care is not always available, still have epidemics of communicable diseases.

Developing vaccines

This timeline shows when certain vaccines were developed.

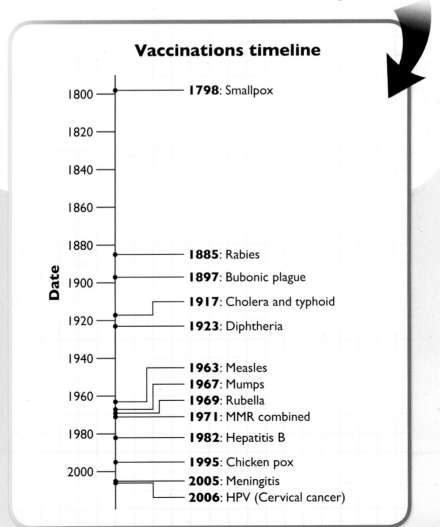

Vaccinations timeline

Date

- **1798**: Smallpox
- **1885**: Rabies
- **1897**: Bubonic plague
- **1917**: Cholera and typhoid
- **1923**: Diphtheria
- **1963**: Measles
- **1967**: Mumps
- **1969**: Rubella
- **1971**: MMR combined
- **1982**: Hepatitis B
- **1995**: Chicken pox
- **2005**: Meningitis
- **2006**: HPV (Cervical cancer)

HEART DISEASE

The heart is the strongest muscle in the human body. Its main job is to pump blood. In one minute, a heart beats 60 to 100 times. That is 30 million beats a year and about 2.5 billion beats in a lifetime. Every day, a healthy heart pumps 7,570 liters (2,000 gallons) of blood through the body. The blood flows along 96,560 km (60,000 miles) of blood vessels. The heart and blood vessels together form the **cardiovascular** system.

People develop cardiovascular problems for many reasons. Most cardiovascular disease is a result of poor diet, lack of exercise, limited medical care, and/or infections.

 This diagram shows the human cardiovascular system (in red and blue). Your heart pumps blood throughout your body using blood vessels.

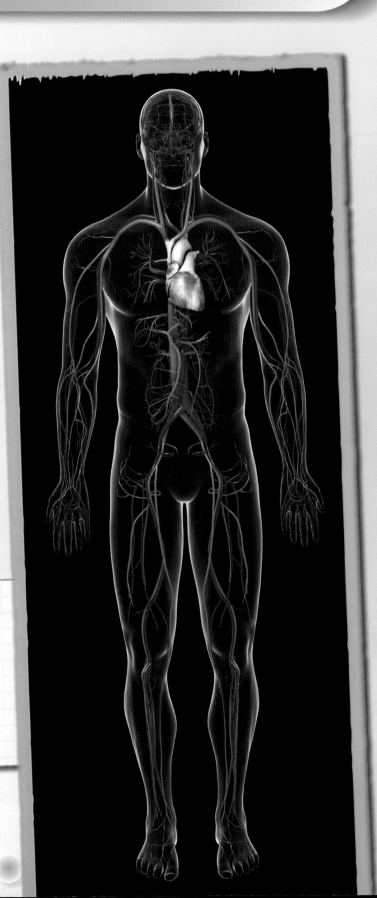

Common heart diseases include coronary heart disease, heart attacks, and strokes. Coronary heart disease happens when blood vessels become clogged from fats or **cholesterol**. When that happens, blood cannot flow through the vessels easily. Clogged blood vessels can also lead to heart attack or stroke. A heart attack happens when blood cannot flow to part of the heart. Stroke happens when blood cannot flow to the brain. Cardiovascular disease is the world's number one killer. Nearly 7 million people a year die from diseased blood vessels. Another 6 million die from strokes.

The high cost of heart disease in Europe

Medical care for heart disease is expensive. In Europe, the cost of heart disease care adds up to nearly $30.6 billion. Total costs for cardiovascular medical care in the United States in 2008 amounted to $296.4 billion.

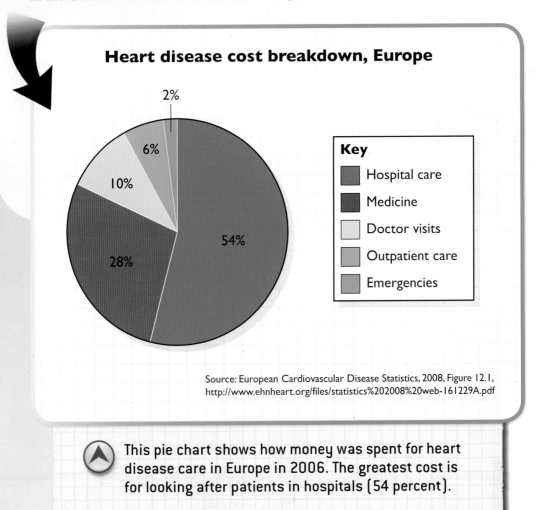

Heart disease cost breakdown, Europe

2%
6%
10%
28%
54%

Key
- Hospital care
- Medicine
- Doctor visits
- Outpatient care
- Emergencies

Source: European Cardiovascular Disease Statistics, 2008, Figure 12.1,
http://www.ehnheart.org/files/statistics%202008%20web-161229A.pdf

This pie chart shows how money was spent for heart disease care in Europe in 2006. The greatest cost is for looking after patients in hospitals (54 percent).

CANCER

Globally, 20,000 people die from cancer every day. Cancer is not one single disease. It is more than 100 different diseases. Cancer happens when cells in the body become **mutated**. Cancer cells grow very quickly and often clump together to form **tumors**. Some cancers begin in one part of the body and then spread to other parts. Cancer diseases are named for the body parts they have affected.

In 2007, 12 million new cancer cases were reported worldwide. Most new cancer cases were in adults. Adults are more likely to get cancer than children.

Men and women get different types of cancer, partly because they have different body parts. In developed countries, the three most common newly diagnosed cancers in men are prostate, lung, and colorectal cancer. Among women, they are breast, colorectal, and lung cancer.

Cancer can be treated through surgery, **chemotherapy**, or **radiation**. Some patients need a combination of treatments. Three out of five cancer patients have the cancer cells or tumors removed by surgery. Chemotherapy is the use of anti-cancer medicines to kill cancer cells. Radiation therapy uses X-rays to damage or destroy cancer cells. Radiation may shrink a tumor or make it go away. When a person's cancer appears to be gone, that person is in **remission**. Doctors test patients in remission for several years to make sure the cancer does not come back.

 One treatment for cancer is chemotherapy.

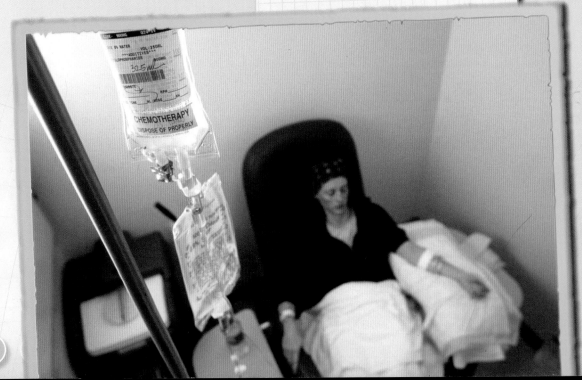

Leukemia

One in four children who develop cancer have leukemia. Leukemia is a cancer where the bone marrow produces a large number of mutated white blood cells, as shown in this photo. These cells do not work properly. They are unable to protect the body from disease. The treatment of children with leukemia is usually a success. About 90 percent of children who have the disease go into remission. The two large circles in this photo are leukemia cells.

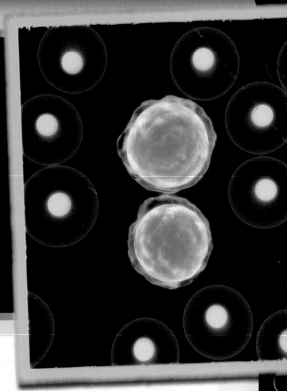

Cancer in men and women

This bar graph compares new cancer cases reported for men and women in 2006. Note that men were diagnosed with lung cancer far more often than women. Men do get breast cancer, but the data is too small to record on this graph. Women do not get prostate cancer because they do not have a prostate gland.

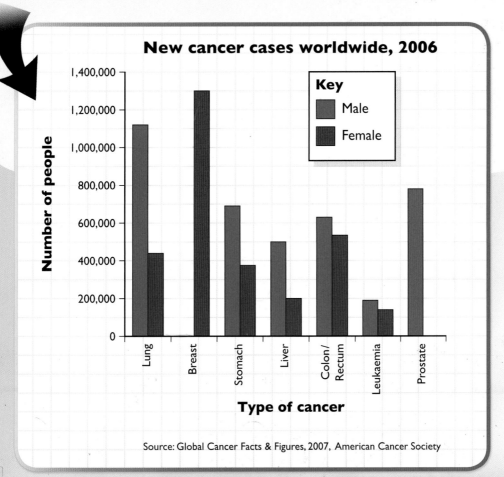

New cancer cases worldwide, 2006

Key
- Male
- Female

Number of people (y-axis: 0, 200,000, 400,000, 600,000, 800,000, 1,000,000, 1,200,000, 1,400,000)

Type of cancer (x-axis: Lung, Breast, Stomach, Liver, Colon/Rectum, Leukaemia, Prostate)

Source: Global Cancer Facts & Figures, 2007, American Cancer Society

DIABETES

Diabetes is a disease that affects how the human body uses **glucose**, the body's main fuel source. When people eat, their bodies turn starches and sugars into glucose. The glucose goes into the bloodstream. Bodies make a chemical called insulin that helps the sugar move from the blood into the body's cells to be converted into energy.

People with Type I diabetes cannot produce insulin. People with Type II diabetes make insulin, but their insulin does not work properly. If glucose cannot go into other cells, it stays in the blood as blood sugar. Too much blood sugar makes the body sick. The most serious problems that arise from diabetes are kidney failure and blindness.

Diabetics treat their disease in different ways. Some people are lucky and can control their diabetes through their diet. For more serious diabetes, patients need to take insulin in pills, shots, or both.

 People with diabetes need to test their blood sugar levels regularly.

The figures

Diabetes is the fourth most common cause of death worldwide. The disease affects 246 million people. It is expected that by 2025, there will be 380 million people with diabetes. But, surprisingly, half the people who have diabetes do not know they have the disease.

Diabetes is a disease seen in people throughout the world. The countries with the most cases are India (40.9 million people affected), China (39.8 million), the U.S. (19.2 million), Russia (9.6 million), and Germany (7.4 million). In some countries, a high percentage of the population has diabetes. The Pacific island nation of Nauru, which lies halfway between Honolulu, Hawaii, and Sydney, Australia, has the highest percentage of diabetics, with 30.7 percent of its population affected. Other nations with high rates of diabetes are in the Middle East: the United Arab Emirates (19.5 percent), Saudi Arabia (16.7 percent), Bahrain (15.2 percent), and Kuwait (14.4 percent).

Treating diabetes

This pie chart shows how people who know they have diabetes treat their condition. Most people (57 percent) take oral medicine. Sixteen percent take no medicine. They treat their diabetes with diet. Only a doctor can say which type of treatment is right for a patient.

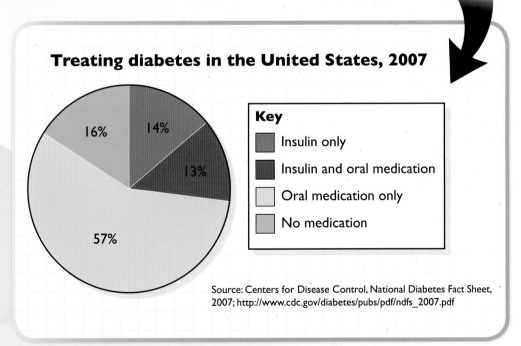

Treating diabetes in the United States, 2007

- 14%
- 13%
- 57%
- 16%

Key
- Insulin only
- Insulin and oral medication
- Oral medication only
- No medication

Source: Centers for Disease Control, National Diabetes Fact Sheet, 2007; http://www.cdc.gov/diabetes/pubs/pdf/ndfs_2007.pdf

An **addiction** is a strong physical urge to do something unhealthy. Tobacco, drugs, and alcohol are addictive substances. They add chemicals to the body. Once a person is addicted, it is hard to stop because the body becomes dependent on those chemicals. Tobacco, drug, and alcohol use also damages body organs and can lead to heart disease, cancer, liver failure, and other serious diseases.

Tobacco use

Tobacco comes in the form of cigarettes, cigars, and chewing tobacco. The addictive chemical in tobacco is called nicotine.

Most teen smokers start using tobacco to look cool or fit in with their friends. They expect to stop smoking within a few years. The truth is that nearly 90 percent of adult smokers started at or before the age of 19. Nicotine is very addictive, so it is very hard for a smoker to quit.

Cigarette smoking causes serious health problems among children and teens. Some experience coughing, shortness of breath, or poor physical fitness. Nearly a third of long-term tobacco users die from a smoking-related disease. Common illnesses include cancer and heart disease.

Smoking and cancer

Tobacco use is related to 15 different types of cancer, including lung, throat, and mouth cancer. Tobacco use is responsible for 30 percent of all cancer deaths and 87 percent of lung cancer deaths.

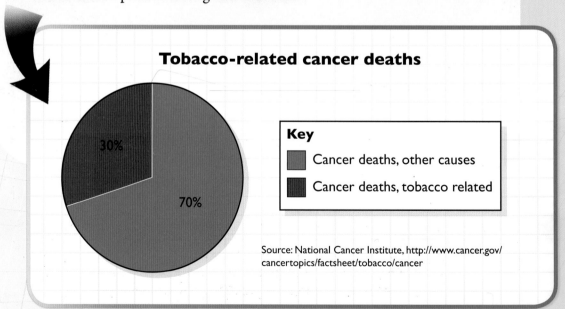

Tobacco-related cancer deaths

30%

70%

Key

Cancer deaths, other causes

Cancer deaths, tobacco related

Source: National Cancer Institute, http://www.cancer.gov/cancertopics/factsheet/tobacco/cancer

 Tobacco is a leading cause of cancer, lung disease, and heart disease.

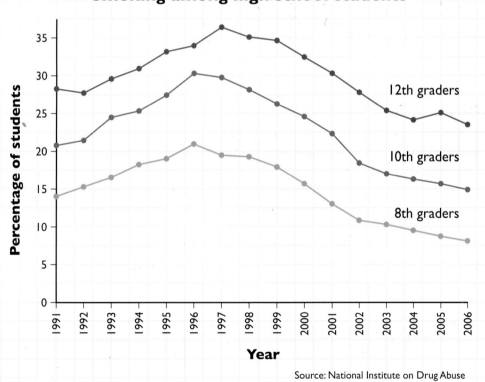

Smoking among high school students

12th graders

10th graders

8th graders

Percentage of students

Year

Source: National Institute on Drug Abuse

 This line graph shows trends over time. In the 1990s, the percentage of teen smokers increased. In the early 2000s, the percentage of student smokers decreased, but it still remains high.

Alcohol and drug use

Worldwide, teen alcohol and drug use is increasing. Children see drug and alcohol use in movies, on television, and in their homes. Some children try drugs and alcohol because their friends offer them the chance to do so. Few teens think about the health problems linked to smoking or drinking.

Alcohol abuse means drinking too much beer, wine, or hard liquor such as vodka. Drug abuse includes excessive or incorrect use of **prescription** drugs or illegal drugs such as marijuana, cocaine, or crack. Alcohol and drugs are both addictive. It is easy to start using these substances, but very difficult to stop. Today, more than 190 million people worldwide are suffering from drug addiction. Many more abuse alcohol.

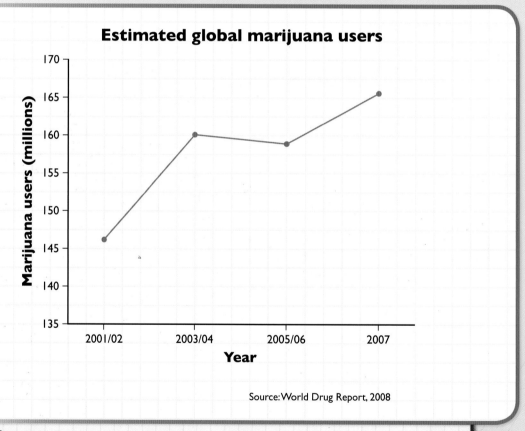

Estimated global marijuana users

Source: World Drug Report, 2008

 This line graph shows the changes in global marijuana use from 2001/2002 through 2007. The number of marijuana users increased by 20 million from 2001 to 2007.

Prescription and over-the-counter drug addiction

Most people think drugs from a drugstore or supermarket are safe to take. If a doctor orders a medicine, people think that is also safe. Those drugs are only safe to take according to the directions. They should be taken for a specific health problem only, and often only for a short time.

It is dangerous to use over-the-counter or prescription medicines without a doctor's care. Abusing prescription and over-the-counter drugs causes damage to the heart, lungs, liver, stomach, and nervous system, just like using illegal drugs does. Prescription and over-the-counter drugs are the second most commonly abused drugs by children ages 12 to 17. The most commonly abused drug is marijuana.

There is a wide range of prescription drugs. Abusing them can be as dangerous as abusing illegal drugs.

EATING DISORDERS

Eating disorders are problems with either eating too much or eating too little over a long period of time. Eating too much may result in **obesity**. Eating too little may be a symptom of **anorexia**. Another eating disorder, **bulimia**, is also called binging and purging. Bulimics eat plenty of food, but they force themselves to vomit what they eat.

People develop eating disorders for many different reasons. They may have had an upsetting event in their life, such as the death of a parent. They may have an unrealistic idea of how they look and worry too much about it. They may have so much unhappiness that they develop eating disorders.

 Obesity may cause serious health issues, including high blood pressure and diabetes.

Each eating disorder has serious effects on the human body. Anorexia is the third most common illness among teens. Ninety-five percent of these are females. People with anorexia may have low blood pressure, an irregular heartbeat, hair loss, brittle bones, or swollen joints. In the worst possible case, anorexics may starve themselves to death. Bulimics risk stomach problems, tooth decay, and damage to their kidneys. People who suffer from obesity may have high blood pressure, damage their bones and joints, or develop diabetes or liver problems.

Obesity

The table below lists obesity rates in a small group of countries. The bar graph shows the same information in a more readable form. Obesity is a real medical issue. People who suffer from obesity struggle to control their weight problems. Medical care for obesity and diseases related to obesity cost billions of dollars.

Country	Percentage of population
United States	30.6%
United Kingdom	23.0%
Australia	21.7%
Spain	13.1%
Denmark	9.5%
Japan	3.2%

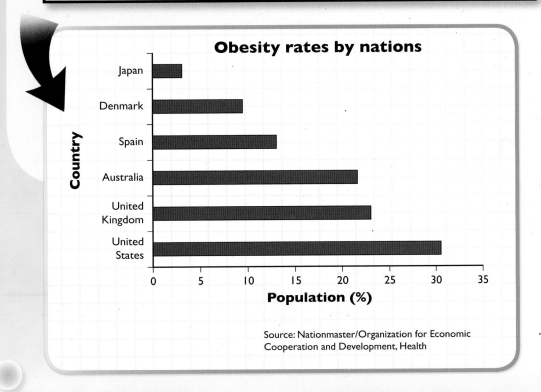

Obesity rates by nations

Source: Nationmaster/Organization for Economic Cooperation and Development, Health

NUTRITION, EXERCISE, AND HYGIENE

Good **nutrition,** exercise, and **hygiene** are vital if you want to stay healthy. We get our nutrients—the natural substances that keep our bodies working—from food. Hygiene is the process of keeping our bodies clean.

People who want to be healthy need to eat healthy foods. Nutrition experts know the human body needs protein, vitamins, fats, carbohydrates, and minerals. Together these substances give our bodies the fuel they need to grow. Not all experts agree on how much of each food group people should eat.

Good nutrition balances a variety of foods from different food groups. Protein-rich foods include meat, fish, poultry, nuts, beans, eggs, and dairy products. Carbohydrates are starches and sugars. They provide energy. Carbohydrate-rich foods include wheat, rice and other grains, and fruits. Dairy products, vegetables, grains, and fruits provide the vitamins and minerals needed for good health.

Healthy fats

Most people think oil and fats are not healthy. Nutritionists know this is not true. We need some fat in our diets, but we need to be careful of the amount and type of fat we eat. Try to only eat "good" fats. Good fats include omega-3 fatty acids (fish, seafood), oil in nuts such as almonds, and liquid oils such as olive oil and canola oil.

 A balanced diet includes fruits, vegetables, grains, dairy, and protein.

Exercise!

In addition to eating healthily, exercise is vital for good health. Exercise keeps muscles toned and strong. It also releases chemicals in the body that make people feel better. Even 15 minutes of exercise has been found to reduce **obesity** among children.

To make exercise more enjoyable, choose an activity you enjoy, such as playing a game of basketball or riding a bicycle. It can also be helpful to add physical activity to daily activities. You could walk to school instead of taking a bus, or climb the stairs instead of taking an elevator.

The Food Pyramid

The U.S. government uses this food pyramid to show the ingredients of a healthy diet. Divided like a pie chart, this pyramid shows the **proportions** of food that you should eat. The person climbing the stairs is a reminder that exercise is also important to keep healthy.

GRAINS   VEGETABLES   FRUITS   MILK   MEAT & BEANS

Hygiene

Good hygiene habits keep our bodies clean and healthy. Such habits include washing our hair, taking a shower or bath, and brushing and flossing our teeth. Being clean is particularly important for students. The top five reasons that students miss school are common colds, stomach flu/diarrhea, ear infections, pink eye, and sore throats. Better hygiene can reduce the spread of these diseases. By keeping our bodies clean we remove germs that will make us and other people sick.

Here are some quick hygiene tips: Wash your hands regularly with soap and water. Wash your hands after using the restroom, before eating or preparing food, and after blowing a runny nose. Trim your nails regularly. This helps prevent hangnails and infected nailbeds. Keep your hands away from your eyes and out of your mouth, especially when people around you have colds or flu.

Wash your hands!

Only five out of ten boys (48 percent) and six out of ten girls (58 percent) in middle school and high school wash their hands after using the bathroom. Of those children, two of the six girls use soap when washing their hands. Of the five boys who washed their hands, only one used soap. Practice good hygiene—wash your hands with soap each time you use the bathroom.

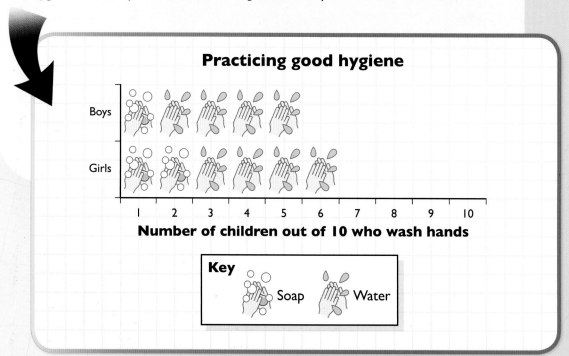

Practicing good hygiene

Boys

Girls

1   2   3   4   5   6   7   8   9   10

Number of children out of 10 who wash hands

Key
Soap   Water

The common cold

Viruses cause colds. Colds are most contagious during the first two to four days after symptoms appear. This is why practicing good hygiene and washing your hands frequently is so important. You may not be able to always recognize who has a cold. Colds spread through the air and by contact with surfaces infected with the virus. Typical symptoms are a runny nose, sore throat, and coughing. People can reduce the chance of spreading a cold by using tissues and throwing them in the trash. There is no cure for the common cold, but better hygiene can reduce the spread of colds.

CHART SMARTS

Data are bits of information about something. We get data as a list of facts or a mass of numbers. It can be difficult to understand large amounts of data. Graphs and charts are ways of displaying information visually. We can see relationships and patterns in data presented in graphs and charts. The type of chart used depends on the data that need to be represented.

Pie charts

A pie chart is used to show the different parts of a whole picture. A pie chart is the best way to show how something is divided up. These charts show information as different sized portions of a circle. They can help you compare **proportions**. You can easily see which section is the largest "slice" of the pie.

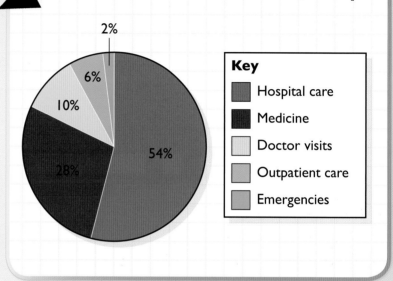

Heart disease cost breakdown, Europe

Key
- Hospital care
- Medicine
- Doctor visits
- Outpatient care
- Emergencies

Line graphs

Line graphs use lines to connect points on a graph. They can be used to show how something changes over time. If you put several lines on one line graph, you can compare the overall pattern of several sets of data.

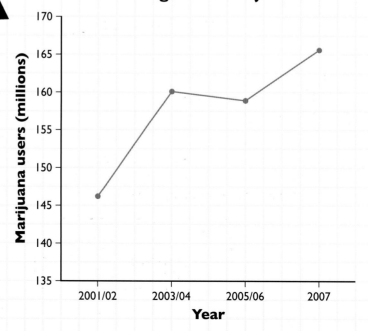

Estimated global marijuana users

Bar graphs

A bar graph is a good way to compare amounts of different things. Bar graphs have a horizontal **x-axis** and a vertical **y-axis**. On this graph, the x-axis shows the items being compared. The y-axis shows the scale of comparison.

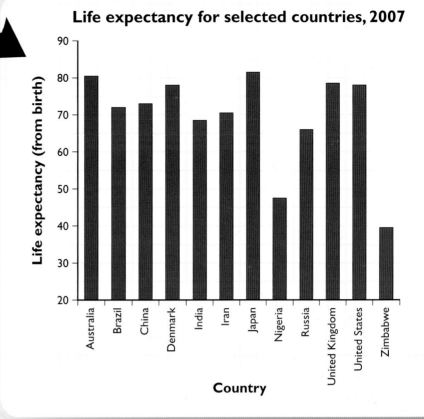

Life expectancy for selected countries, 2007

Pictograms

A pictogram uses pictures or icons to represent information in a graph. A pictogram might represent people, animals, plants, or items, such as pills or hospitals. A pictogram should have an explanation of what each icon stands for.

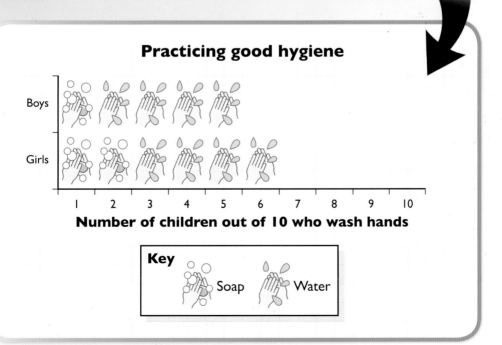

Practicing good hygiene

Number of children out of 10 who wash hands

GLOSSARY

addiction hard-to-stop dependence on a substance

anorexia serious loss of appetite to the point of starvation

antibody protein that fights germs that cause disease

bacteria extremely small organisms that can only be seen through a microscope

Black Death plague that was one of the worst epidemics in world history

bulimia eating disorder in which people eat food, then intentionally vomit

cardiovascular related to the heart and blood vessels (veins and arteries)

cell building block of all living things

chemotherapy cancer-fighting treatment

cholesterol compound of fat and alcohol found in most body tissues

communicable disease spread from one person to another

congenital referring to a condition or disease that a person is born with

contagious disease that has a tendency to spread among people

dehydration having too little water

developed country country where many people are relatively well-off and many work in offices or in new technology, rather than producing food or raw materials

developing country country where many people have little money and most work producing food or raw materials

epidemic outbreak of a disease in a large number of people within a population at the same time

gene part of a cell that controls the characteristics you get from your parents

glucose carbohydrate (sugar) that is used by human cells for energy

hygiene activities that promote and preserve good health through cleanliness

immunization making a human or animal immune to a specific disease

infect when a disease-causing germ enters and grows in a body

inherit receive from a parent or relative

life expectancy how long a person is expected to live for

microbe tiny form of life that can only be seen under a microscope

mutate change the genetic material of a cell

non-communicable not spread through person-to-person or other contact

nutrition study of food and how the body uses that food

obesity excessive amount of body fat

organ part of the body that does a particular job

prescription doctor's order for medicine

proportion size of a group of data compared to other groups, or to the whole set of data

protein substance found in some foods which living things need to grow new cells

radiation x-ray particles used to damage or destroy cancer cells

remission temporary recovery from an illness

semen body fluid from male reproductive glands

tuberculosis bacterial disease that usually infects the lungs

tumor abnormal growth and clumping together of cells

urine liquid body waste

vaccine medicine that encourages antibodies to form in the body to prevent disease

virus minute living organisms that cause disease

x-axis horizontal line on a graph

y-axis vertical line on a graph

FURTHER INFORMATION

Books

Claybourne, Anna. *Healthy Eating: Diet and Nutrition*. Chicago: Heinemann Library, 2008.

DeGezelle, Terri. *The Real Deal: Illness*. Chicago: Heinemann Library, 2009.

Giddens, Sandra. *Making Smart Choices about Food, Nutrition, and Lifestyle*. New York: Rosen Central, 2008.

Marcovitz, Hal. *Drug and Alcohol Abuse.* Broomall, PA.: Mason Crest Library, 2007.

Miller, Edward. *The Monster Health Book: A Guide to Eating Healthy, Being Active & Feeling Great for Monsters & Kids*. NY: Holiday House Books, 2008.

Silverstein, Alvin, Virginia B. Silverstein, and Laura Silverstein Nunn. *The Eating Disorders Update: Understanding Anorexia, Bulimia, and Binge Eating*. Berkeley Heights, NJ: Enslow Publishing, 2008.

Simons, Rae. *AIDS & HIV: The Facts for Kids*. Vestal, NY: AlphaHouse Publishing, 2008.

Websites

Full, detailed explanations of the human body, illnesses, conditions, and how to maintain a healthy body.
http://kidshealth.org

WebMD is for adults, but they have an extensive site that talks about children's health. You can find information on babies, children, and teens, including 40 health tips for kids.
http://children.webmd.com/

This website offers information on diseases, medicine, and healthy living. There is a section that includes Frequently Asked Questions (FAQs) and provides answers about health issues in children.
http://www.netdoctor.co.uk/children/index.shtml

INDEX